REVENUE MANAGEMENT MADE EASY
For Midscale and Limited-Service Hotels

The 6 Strategic Steps for Becoming the Most Valuable Person at Your Property

by Ira Vouk

March 31st, 2018
San Diego, CA

ISBN: 978-1-387-70254-1

All rights reserved
©Ira Vouk Revenue Management Services
Reprints and/or electronic distribution
is not permitted without written authorization

Edited by Jeremiah Magone

In 1992 Bill Scatchard wrote 'Upsetting the Apple Cart: A common sense approach to successful hotel operations for the 1990's'. That book helped many middle-tier hotel operators, including me, become better hoteliers.

But that was 25 years ago... when words like 'rate transparency', 'rate parity', 'OTAs', 'electronic rate distribution', 'yield management', and even the term 'revenue manager' weren't even in our lexicon...

A lot has changed since then. That's why there needs to be a new set of principles written for the modern era, to help guide revenue managers down the most profitable path for each individual hotel. In 'Revenue Management Made Easy', Ira Vouk aims to do just that.

So, if you want to make your hotel more financially successful... If you want to increase your hotel's top and bottom line revenue... If you want to become the most valuable person at your hotel property... Then read, absorb and implement Ira's Revenue Management strategies. All the tools you need to become the revenue manager everyone wants to hire are in this book.

It's time for you to 'upset the Revenue Management applecart' at your hotel, so you can start discovering new opportunities for driving your revenues and your career to new levels.

Dana Blasi
President,
Gaslamp Hotel Management, Inc.

CONTENTS

Introduction	6
What makes a next-level revenue manager?	8
Specifics of managing room inventory	10
The main indexes used in the revenue management science	15
Adjusted RevPAR (ARPAR) as a new performance metric that reflects the bottom line	18
6 easy steps to successful revenue management	25
STEP 1: DYNAMIC PRICING	26
The 2 types of data needed for successful dynamic pricing	28
Mistake 1: pricing based on occupancy	33
Mistake 2: pricing based on competition	40
STEP 2: SETTING STAY RESTRICTIONS	46
STEP 3: MANAGING BOOKING CHANNELS	49
Your first 3 steps for optimizing revenues, visualized	52
STEP 4: OVERSELLING	54
STEP 5: MANAGING GROUP AND CORPORATE BUSINESS	63
STEP 6: MARKETING	66
Other tactics for increasing revenue	69
Managing online reviews	69
Upgrading	70
Managing room type differentials	71
Managing ancillary revenues	72
Review	73
Automation in hospitality revenue management	75
Summary	77
Glossary	81

INTRODUCTION

Why does revenue need to be managed? This seems like a rhetorical question, but you'll be surprised to know that only a very small portion of mid-tier US hotels implement adequate Revenue Management strategies in their daily operations. That means the vast majority aren't using any kind of Revenue Management strategies whatsoever, dramatically limiting their properties' revenue potential. So reading this book and implementing what I'm about to show you in these pages will already differentiate you from the majority of hoteliers, and give you what you need, to **add an additional 10%-20% in top-line revenue to your hotel's profitability.** For a 100-room hotel property, this can translate into $200,000-$400,000 or more in revenue each year.

And even if you're already using some Revenue Management strategies, I'm sure you realize that the hospitality industry (and hospitality Revenue Management, in particular) is a very dynamic environment. Things change very quickly and so do the strategies and tactics that make a hotelier successful. This is due to the fact that consumers are getting smarter every day, and the tools they use to travel are becoming more diverse and sophisticated. So even though the core concepts of Revenue Management remain the same, this dynamic environment dictates the necessity to constantly review and refresh the actual tactics you're using in your daily Revenue Management routine.

That's why this book was created to bring a fresh view on Hospitality Revenue Management and describe the tools that are relevant and effective today. After you start applying these strategies – I can promise you that in less than a month you'll start noticing the difference.

This book contains both theoretical knowledge (using simple and clear explanations) and practical advice (including specific steps and examples) on how to Revenue Manage your hotel and significantly grow your RevPAR and your bottom line. You'll get insider tips, such as: how to properly implement dynamic pricing, how to look at your STR report to make sure your occupancy rates are balanced with your ADR, and the proper way to use overbooking to grow your revenue during periods of peak demand. Do this right and you'll be able to achieve great results in no time.

So whether you are a professional certified Revenue Manager, a GM looking to improve your hotel's RevPAR or a student searching for additional knowledge on this discipline – this book will help you become more knowledgeable and more successful.

WHAT MAKES A NEXT-LEVEL REVENUE MANAGER?

REVENUE MANAGEMENT IS A SET OF STRATEGIES that help realize optimal revenues and profits for capacity-constrained and perishable assets (hotel rooms, in our case). The key word in this definition is 'optimal', because this is what separates basic Revenue Management from next-level revenue generation. To make that distinction in your career, you need the skills, which will help you provide the right service to the right customer at the right time for the right price – by understanding, anticipating and influencing consumer behavior through demand forecasts. Unfortunately, some Revenue Managers believe they're already doing this by following their competitors' rates (compset), chasing after occupancy goals, or accepting every piece of group business that comes their way. However, these strategies no are no longer efficient because we now live in a very dynamic environment.

Today, hospitality market presents a high level of uncertainty, because we don't know:

- How strong the demand will be on any given day in the future
- What the price expectations of those customers will be
- What competitors will implement today, tomorrow and every day in the future
- How future events will affect revenues (for example, economic situation, changes in gas prices or air fares, construction next door, etc.)

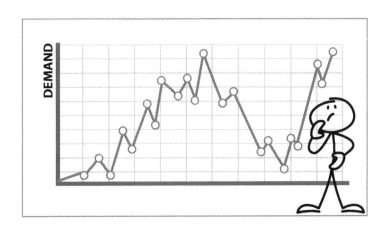

While no one can see the future, being a next-level Revenue Manager means you've always got your eye on the ever-changing demand levels for your specific property, and you're ready to adjust yourself to the changing situation at a moment's notice.

The market is more dynamic than ever before, after all. Customers are now equipped with a wide range of tools that help them uncover deals on numerous OTAs, opaque and aggregator websites that don't always contribute to the hotels' revenue growth. All this has a direct impact on your bottom line, for good or for ill, depending on how well you're following your market.

As Mr. Blasi said in the forward to this book, times have changed. Yes... No longer can you just 'set it and forget it'. No longer can you base your prices on foliage or the shape of the moon. Hoteliers who continue following those practices will also continue losing revenue every day. In order to succeed in this new marketplace, every single hotel needs to understand the value of adequate proactive daily Revenue Management.

That means **planning and forecasting demand for every single day in the future (at least 365 days ahead) and then staying flexible enough to change your strategy when need be.**

That's how you keep yourself from going down with too many unsold rooms on the day of arrival or selling out all your rooms at lower rates than the market was willing to bear. These are a few of the business advantages **Dynamic Pricing** will give you, which we will discuss in detail further throughout this book.

One more thing to keep in mind before moving forward: hotel rooms are different from most other products on the market because of their perishable nature - they cannot be resold once they've expired for the day. This is why it's very important to correctly react to demand fluctuations, follow your booking pace, select the right strategy and act accordingly. The following chapter provides more details regarding the specifics of managing this kind of product.

SPECIFICS OF MANAGING ROOM INVENTORY

TO BECOME THE MOST IMPORTANT PERSON AT YOUR HOTEL, you need to see that Revenue Management techniques are dictated by the type of product you're selling. So let's start by asking: what makes managing hotel room inventory different from, say, selling apples at the local grocery store?

1. Perishability

The average shelf life of an average apple is 2-4 weeks (yes, I was surprised, too). So even though apples are considered 'perishable', you've got up to 28 days to sell them.

Hotel rooms, airline tickets, car rental, or anything else that is rented by the month, day, hour, or second, on the other hand, is considered **highly perishable**.

After all, you only have 1 chance to rent a hotel room for the 4th of July. After the end of that day, your inventory instantly goes bad and you have to 'take it off the shelf' and display a new offer called 'July 5th' (which is normally much less valuable).

2. Strictly limited supply

Another limitation with hotel inventory is that you can't adjust your supply according to demand forecast the way you could if you were selling apples. You can only sell X number of hotel rooms (or less, if a few of your rooms are out of order because you're fixing that bed bug issue) at any given point in time. Hence, we need to take a different strategy when managing this kind of product, which will be described below.

That is why, unlike other markets, where supply can be easily fluctuated, the travel industry often experiences situations when demand exceeds supply. This has resulted in an overflow, which explains the tremendous success of the short-term vacation rental market (aka 'alternative lodging') in recent years. But that is a whole separate discussion…

3. Selling the promise

Another characteristic of extreme perishability is that you need to start selling your rooms before they're even available because it's nearly impossible to fill a property by only accepting walk-in guests on the day of arrival.

You do that by selling the promise, not the actual product (unlike an apple on the shelf in a store). This is why it's important for you to have a Revenue Management plan for selling your rooms 365 days (or even more) in advance.

4. Overselling

Sometimes you can (and you should) sell more promises than you can deliver! Known as overselling (or overbooking), this is a technique used in Revenue Management to offset anticipated cancellations and no-shows. Proper overselling at the peak of demand helps hoteliers sell their inventory at the premium rate and not leave money on the table from empty rooms. This is an optimal strategy, which leads to revenue (and profit) maximization. The additional revenues gained from overselling go straight to the bottom line.

Later on, I'll show you the precise strategies to do this successfully. Learn this and watch your ownership beam with pride as you reach 100% occupancy without having to lower your ADR in the slightest.

Managing hotel rooms

So based on what we discussed above, what are the specifics of Revenue Managing this kind of product?

With apples, you maximize your profits through sophisticated logistics and fluctuating Supply (with relatively fixed prices) based on your demand forecast, as shown on the graph below:

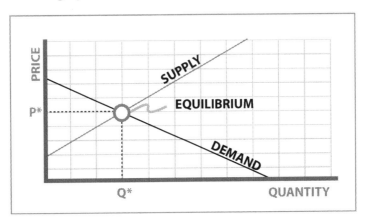

With hotel rooms, on the other hand, **since supply is a fixed variable** (as we discussed earlier in this chapter), **all you have left to fluctuate is your pricing, based on the demand fluctuations.** Thus, price is determined entirely by demand conditions. Here is how that relationship looks, when graphed:

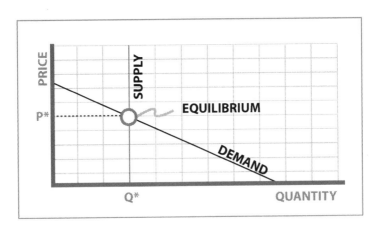

The concept is as follows: **in general, when demand is strong, your pricing should go up to improve your Average Daily Rate (ADR); when demand is weak, prices should go down to increase occupancy.** This is called **'Dynamic Pricing'** and the idea is about as basic as it gets. However, in practice, this is what helps us make smart, real-time adjustments to demand fluctuations in the market so we're constantly optimizing our rates for maximum revenue production – and that's one of the most powerful tactics in Revenue Management.

As a practical example of this approach, back in 1999, the Coca Cola Company decided to create a vending machine with a built-in thermometer that raised the price of Coke in hot weather. Since the machine only held 100 cans (it had a fixed, limited supply), it was obvious that the only way to increase revenue was to fluctuate the price based on changes in demand.

Even though that was nearly 20 years ago, the majority of small- to mid-sized hotels still aren't implementing even these basic Revenue Management strategies. This is unfortunate, because there have been multiple times in my career when I've gone into a hotel, implemented Dynamic Pricing and helped them grow their top line revenue by 20% in just a few months. **And all it takes is 30 minutes a day over your morning coffee.** That's why I wrote this book - to show you how easy Revenue Management really is. If you just follow the steps I've laid out, you'll be performing the same kind of 'revenue miracles' at your property, as well.

Again, proper pricing adjustments (daily or even hourly), which take existing demand into account, is the key to increased profitability. In a perfect scenario, on any given day, you need to:

- sell 100% of your available inventory;
- do so at a maximum potential price;
- and with minimum expenses (in commissions and fees).

And due to the specifics of the product, you accomplish these goals by **starting to sell your inventory (or 'the promise') 365 days in advance according to predicted demand, by constantly fluctuating your price in a way that allows** you to reach the highest occupancy with the highest possible ADR, and sometimes overselling in anticipation of cancelations and no-shows.

Those are the specific Revenue Management techniques that are dictated by the characteristics of 'hotel rooms' as a product. They should be applied on a day-by-day basis in order to maximize profits.

THE MAIN INDEXES USED IN THE REVENUE MANAGEMENT SCIENCE

LET'S START MOVING ON FROM THEORY TO PRACTICE. To do that, you need to know, which Revenue Management metrics to focus on and when, and what kind of conclusions you should draw from each, so you're always making the best revenue decisions. This section is where you will learn how to accurately measure the success of your strategy at any point in time and, thus, ensure your hotel's long-term profitability.

Occupancy

Occupancy is the percentage of all rental units in the hotel that are occupied at a given time.

We calculate this as:

*The number of occupied rooms/
The number of total available rooms*

This is expressed as a percentage.

ADR (average daily rate)

ADR is the average rental rate per occupied room in a given time period.

This is calculated as:

Room revenue/The number of rooms sold

This is expressed in monetary units.

As a side note, many times a hotel's success is evaluated based on one of the indexes mentioned above (more often – occupancy). Unfortunately, this limited analysis doesn't reflect the complexity of the relationship between these two indexes and the sales volumes they generate.

So, a while back Revenue Managers introduced a more accurate coefficient of measurement – RevPAR – which combines the two, occupancy and ADR, in one statistic.

RevPAR (revenue per available room)

RevPAR has been used as the key metric to measure a hotel's productivity and to compare that property with different properties in a market.

It can be calculated in a few different ways:

$$RevPAR = ADR \times Occupancy$$
or
$$RevPAR = Total\ guest\ room\ revenue/$$
$$The\ number\ of\ total\ available\ rooms/$$
$$The\ number\ of\ days\ in\ the\ period$$

RevPAR allows for obtaining a more accurate and broad picture of your hotel's performance, and also to compare the results with competitors in your market. It is recommended that a hotel signs up to receive monthly STR reports, also called 'STAR reports', which display a property's performance compared to other hotels in the area.

Unfortunately, RevPAR is still not the most accurate index for measuring the effectiveness of your hotel's Revenue Management activities, regardless of the widely spread opinion in the hotel industry. This statistic doesn't objectively reflect the performance (and profitability) of your hotel or particular Revenue Management techniques, for the following reasons:

- It doesn't take CPOR (costs per occupied room) into account. If you don't know

this you might sell out your rooms at a low ADR, ultimately hurting your profits (even though it may seem like you're increasing your top line).
- It doesn't consider any additional income a hotel may have from other revenue-generating departments, such as: restaurants, meeting space, banquet rooms, casinos, parking, spa, etc.

To get a clear view of these metrics – so you have a much more accurate picture of how well you're doing in any given month and know, which corrections to make in your Revenue Management strategy – I developed another, more accurate index, called 'Adjusted RevPAR (ARPAR)' that has been embraced by hospitality professionals all over the world.

Adjusted RevPAR (ARPAR)

Unlike traditional RevPAR, ARPAR reflects the bottom line profits, not just top line revenue. This is incredibly useful for helping us understand the effectiveness of our Revenue Management strategy. And this focus is right in line with the lodging industry's general shift from high-occupancy Revenue Management strategies to those that maximize profits.

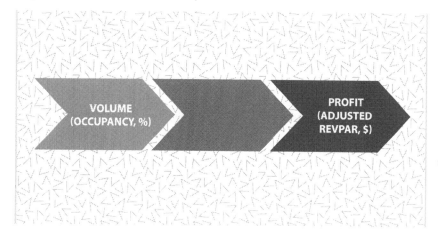

This metric is calculated as follows:

ARPAR = (ADR – The variable costs per occupied room + Additional revenue per occupied room) x Occupancy

The following section describes ARPAR in more detail.

ADJUSTED REVPAR (ARPAR) AS A NEW PERFORMANCE METRIC THAT REFLECTS THE BOTTOM LINE

AS A CONTRAST WITH ADJUSTED REVPAR, let's first look at one mistake that can be made when just using traditional RevPAR to inform your decisions.

For the sake of clarity, we'll look at 2 extreme scenarios:

> A hotel has 100 rooms.
> *Scenario 1:*
> 100 rooms sold at $10 each
> Revenue = $1000
> RevPAR = $10

> *Scenario 2:*
> 10 rooms sold at $100 each
> Revenue = $1000
> RevPAR = $10

Question: If RevPAR is the same in both cases – then why do we have the feeling that Scenario 2 is much more profitable for the hotel? This goes to show that RevPAR is not the most perfect index for measuring a hotel's actual productivity (or, the implemented Revenue Management and pricing strategy, to be exact). To get closer to this goal, Adjusted RevPAR includes additional revenues and takes the variable costs of occupying each room into consideration. You can calculate ARPAR in a few different ways (depending on what measurements you want to use in your calculations):

$$ARPAR = (\text{Room Revenue} + \text{Other Revenues} - \text{Variable costs per occupied room} \times \text{The number of occupied rooms}) / \text{The total number of rooms available for sale}$$

Or:

*ARPAR = (Room Revenue / The number of
occupied rooms + Other Revenues /
The number of occupied rooms −
Variable costs per occupied room) x Occupancy*

Or:

*ARPAR = [Room Revenue / The number of
occupied rooms + Other Revenues / The number of
occupied rooms − Variable costs per
occupied room) x The number of occupied rooms]
/ (The number of rooms at the hotel x
The number of days in the period)*

But the simplest way to express ARPAR is the following:

**ARPAR = (ADR − Variable costs per occupied
room + Additional revenue per occupied room)
x Occupancy**

It can be calculated fairly easily, as soon as you measure your average variable expenses (per occupied room) based on historical accounting data as well as average additional income (per occupied room) from other revenue-generating departments (if any). These values can then be considered constant and used for any future calculations. And recalculation is only needed after dramatic changes at the property, which might significantly affect variable costs or additional revenues.

Now let's apply this formula to the above mentioned scenarios. And for simplicity of calculations, let's assume we're talking about a limited-service hotel that doesn't have any additional revenue-generating departments, and variable expenses are equal to $10 per occupied room.

> **_Scenario 1:_**
> 100 rooms sold at $10 each
> Revenue = $1000
> RevPAR = $10
> Adjusted RevPAR = ($10-$10)*1 = $0
> Profit = ($0 * 100 rooms sold) or
> ($0 * 100 inventory) = $0

> **_Scenario 2:_**
> 10 rooms sold at $100 each
> Revenue = $1000
> RevPAR = $10
> Adjusted RevPAR = ($100 - $10)*0.1 = $9
> Profit = ($90 * 10 rooms sold) or
> ($9 * 100 inventory) = $900

With the results of this example, we can see why we had a feeling, from the very beginning, that the second scenario was much more profitable for the hotel.

RevPAR doesn't give us any information about the real profitability of a property, while ARPAR is a clear reflection of the 'true bottom line profit'.

At this point, we should conclude that concentrating on just maximizing RevPAR can lead to significant profit losses, since sometimes an increase in revenue may actually mean a decrease in final profits. But if you set **ARPAR** maximization as your main goal – it will be much easier for you to make decisions, which lead to an increase in your bottom line, much to your ownership's delight.

Thus, RevPAR growth does not always equal Profit growth (as in the example of high occupancy and low ADR, which involves higher expenses). But at the same time, ARPAR growth will always involve growth in your RevPAR index, which will reflect in your STAR report.

RevPAR, ARPAR and GOPPAR

The hospitality industry has been offering a few other indexes in the recent years that have been trying to compete with RevPAR. All of them are great, but each is limited by a particular area of application. Of these, it's still my opinion that **ARPAR is the most objective and accurate index to use as the target for maximization, as well as to measure the Revenue Manager's performance, overall effectiveness of the property's Revenue Management strategy and pricing policy.**

That said, some readers may be familiar with GOPPAR, and you might be wondering what the differences are between these two metrics.

Simply put, GOPAR is not the same as ARPAR, for the following reasons:

1. First, GOPPAR takes into account all the operating and departmental costs, not just variable costs, so hotel owners can understand how their properties perform in general. But since those costs have less to do with occupancy (and may include things which you, as a Revenue Manager, are not directly responsible for, such as: your Internet bill, or the purchase of new furniture for the hotel), that makes this metric much less helpful in seeing how much your strategy adds to the bottom line.

When calculating ARPAR, it's crucial you only take into account **variable** costs. This allows you to always correctly answer the question of whether to occupy a room at a given rate or not. You can make a wrong decision if you're using GOPPAR as your key metric, since it includes fixed expenses, which ends up setting the bar higher than need be. **Remember, you still incur fixed costs even if the room remains unoccupied.** But since the only ADDITIONAL costs that come with occupied rooms are variable costs, **that's the only standard we need to meet in order to add to the bottom line.**

In other words, GOPPAR can help hotel owners understand how their properties are performing in general, but won't assess the effectiveness of your Revenue Management strategies, specifically.

2. On top of that, GOPPAR cannot be used as a target variable that needs to be maximized because it is retroactive: total property costs are not known until the actual accounting reports are populated. So it's simply not possible to chase GOPAR as a key performance indicator of Revenue Management success.

ARPAR addresses these issues by taking into account the revenues from all departments and only adding variable expenses that are calculated based on the historical cost data, which can be used as a constant for future calculations. Thus ARPAR can also be used in forecasts and as a target for maximization. **When you make maximizing ARPAR your ultimate goal, RevPAR and GOPPAR will increase as a result.**

Here's an example of that point:

> Same 100-room hotel.
> Variable costs per room = $10
> Total operating expenses per room = $40
> And for the simplicity of calculations,
> we aren't going to add any additional revenue
> from other departments.

Now let's take a look at a spreadsheet of what our profits will look like at different ADRs and occupancy levels, according to GOPAR and ARPAR:

Sold rms	Occupancy	ADR	Revenue	RevPAR	GOPPAR	ARPAR	Profit
10	10.00%	$100.00	$1,000	$10.00	$6.00	$9.00	$900.00
11	11.11%	$90.00	$1,000	$10.00	$5.56	$8.89	$888.89
13	12.50%	$80.00	$1,000	$10.00	$5.00	$8.75	$875.00
14	14.29%	$70.00	$1,000	$10.00	$4.29	$8.57	$857.14
17	16.67%	$60.00	$1,000	$10.00	$3.33	$8.33	$833.33
20	20.00%	$50.00	$1,000	$10.00	$2.00	$8.00	$800.00
25	25.00%	$40.00	$1,000	$10.00	$0.00	$7.50	$750.00
33	33.33%	$30.00	$1,000	$10.00	($3.33)	$6.67	$666.67
50	50.00%	$20.00	$1,000	$10.00	($10.00)	$5.00	$500.00
100	100.00%	$10.00	$1,000	$10.00	($30.00)	$0.00	$0.00

According to this spreadsheet, if a Revenue Manager is making a decision on whether or not to occupy a room at a certain room rate, their decision, based on GOPPAR, would look like this:

But if they are basing their decision on ARPAR, this would be their decision-making process:

As you can see, the difference between the two scenarios is **$25 of pure profit in favor of the ARPAR strategy.** Using GOPPAR as the basis for your Revenue Management and pricing strategy, on the other hand, requires turning down any business with rates lower than the Total CPOR (Cost Per Occupied Room). In other words: all reservations with a $40+ rate are good, and everything below that is considered not profitable and is, thus, declined. The big problem with this approach is that you still have to pay **fixed costs, even if the room is unoccupied, so this decision ends up hurting your bottom line.**

And since this is just a single reservation, this difference could add up to thousands of dollars of additional or lost profit for your property, depending on which metric you choose. That's why variable expenses, and not fixed expenses, is where we need to draw the line when we're deciding on whether to accept a reservation, because **any revenues generated by the occupied room that exceed variable expenses go directly to the bottom line.**

There are a few conditions, however, that one needs to take into account when using the ARPAR index:

- While the hotel industry still hasn't come to an agreement in regard to a standard formula for CPOR (cost per occupied room), it's even less clear how exactly to separate variable expenses from fixed. But the good news is:

    - even a rough approximation is good enough and helps achieve great results when used in the ARPAR formula to maximize profits

    - you only need to calculate these variable expenses once for your hotel (and then you can use the same number for all future calculations)

- ARPAR should be used to track your hotel's performance internally. To make comparisons with other hotels you'll have to rely on RevPAR.

To conclude this section, there are a variety of performance metrics that Revenue Managers use, to understand the success of their hotels on any given day, and to guide their Dynamic Rate strategy. But, when we're concerned with whether your Revenue Management strategy is adding to the bottom line or hurting it, Adjusted RevPAR gives you a much clearer picture than any other metric. Knowing this will help you make better decisions and generate more consistent revenues going forward.

6 EASY STEPS TO SUCCESSFUL REVENUE MANAGEMENT

NOW THAT WE KNOW, WHICH METRICS WE SHOULD FOCUS ON, let's discuss the 6 basic steps to successfully growing the bottom line at midscale or limited-service properties. These steps are listed in the order of importance (i.e., projected revenue potential), so I recommend you start with #1 and proceed to the next as you become more comfortable with each tactic in your Revenue Management routine.

STEP 1:
DYNAMIC PRICING

THE FIRST STEP IS TO CREATE A DYNAMIC PRICING STRATEGY. In this section, we'll do this by going through several strategic exercises to arrive at the most profitable decisions for a variety of situations.

The first decision we need to make is around the topic of forecasting. In order to be successful, **it's necessary for you to be able to estimate the approximate demand level at your hotel for every day in the future, at least 365 days ahead, and price your rooms accordingly.** Then, we need to **review these decisions regularly** so you're always able to adjust your room rates (daily or even hourly) based on the demand fluctuations you see. This is the only way you'll be able to implement a successful Dynamic Pricing strategy.

So how do I find the right price to charge? The basic concept behind Dynamic Pricing in Revenue Management is simple: **a hotel room should be priced based on supply and demand inter-correlations (equilibrium price). Supply is a fixed variable when we look at a single property level (as discussed earlier).** That means that all we have to do is watch demand.

This necessitates us to treat:

- each calendar day as a separate season
- each forecast as another opportunity to re-adjust our rates in accordance with the demand fluctuations

These are the 2 general rules for increasing revenue through Dynamic Pricing. Here, notice that maximizing occupancy doesn't make the list. That's because **the ultimate goal of any Revenue Manager should not be increasing occupancy, but rather maximizing the profits, the bottom line.**

Again, we do this by increasing room rates when demand exceeds supply (in order to capitalize on ADR) and lowering rates when demand is weak (in order to increase occupancy).

Another point to consider with Dynamic Pricing is that a Revenue Manager's pricing decisions have long-term effects. If you quickly sell a significant portion of your inventory at a low price, for example, then of course your occupancy index will increase. But that might also mean missing the opportunity to make more money, on more profitable clients, during the days closer to arrival. This is what's known as 'opportunity cost'.

And vice versa, if you hold your prices too high without paying attention to the competitors' prices and a slowdown in the booking pace – this will lead to a situation when a lot of inventory remains unsold. That makes **reviewing your Dynamic Pricing on a regular basis *the* most important thing you do** in all your daily hotel operations.

THE 2 TYPES OF DATA NEEDED FOR SUCCESSFUL DYNAMIC PRICING

AS WE ALREADY KNOW, the main goal of Revenue Management is to *sell the right product to the right customer at the right time and for the right price*, with an ultimate goal of maximizing the bottom line (the final profits). 'The right price' is found through Dynamic Pricing, which should be the central element of every property's Revenue Management strategy.

The next logical question is: **how do we properly track demand?** There are various data points that can be collected to assess demand fluctuations for any given day in the future, but in general, they can be grouped into 2 main categories:

1. 'Macro' level – external market data (in the form of published rates of all hotels in the area/region, as well as observed volume of searches/bookings for future dates in this region). Published rate information can be obtained through various rate shopping tools. There's no shortage of those in the market right now. OTAs also have vast amounts of this data and they're now willing to share this information with their partners and individual hotels.

2. 'Micro' level – internal hotel data (in the form of daily statistics, booking pace, etc.). This data is only available at the hotel level, through access to the property's PMS system.

Micro data can then be broken down further, into 2 categories:

a. *Static data*, which represents a one-dimensional 'snapshot' of a property's current condition (occupancy level, ADR, RevPAR, OOO rooms, groups, etc.) for any given date in the past (final end-of-day numbers) or in the future (current state, on-the-books).

b. *Dynamic data*, which is more informative and volumetric. It describes what happened during some period of time and how the property has reached the current state. It is more like a 'historic video' rather than a snapshot. An example of such data is booking pace (or pickup dynamics), which reflects the speed of sales. This data can also be obtained for past as well as future dates that already have reservations on the books.

There's also the third kind of data many hoteliers refer to when speaking about Dynamic Pricing. I call it 'the noise'. It includes: weather conditions, reputation scores, gas prices, air fares... The list is long but what these items have in common is the following: if you try to take any of those into account, you'll just end up distorting your calculations. Sure, these factors do affect the equilibrium market price, but their impact is already reflected in the two data types above, so no need to count them twice.

Let's take a closer look at the micro and macro data at your property, to understand what you should really focus on.

External market data

The OTAs have vast amounts of *external market data*, like: detailed information about published prices for any day in the future, and assessments of market demand strength, based on search and booking volumes. This is what normally goes in the algorithms that are built in their pricing intelligence tools to calculate the recommended room rates. However, if used alone, without consideration of your internal hotel data points, this data can't provide adequate pricing guidance. **'Compset-oriented pricing' is quite far from the optimal strategy you should be using when making Revenue Management decisions.**

To understand this, there are a few questions you have to ask yourself:

- Have you picked the right compset for your property?
- Do your competitors really know what they're doing? Are you willing to risk falling into a 'blind leading the blind' scenario?
- And, what IS the right compset? Since there, really, is no such thing.

Remember, your compset changes from day to day, and from season to season. Your competitors also change based on the market segment you're in (for example, leisure travelers will consider one set of hotels, and convention attendees will review a whole different set of properties, so what should you do if your property is a representative of both?).

Please don't misunderstand, compset data plays a big role in Revenue Management decisions (logically, those prices are what form the market situation at any given moment). **But one should never ignore the importance of internal hotel data like booking pace, group business on the books, number of vacant rooms, etc. It is impossible to build an optimal pricing strategy without having this data on hand.**

Internal property data

As discussed above, it is important to be aware of the rates your competitors are publishing for any given day in the future. However, in many cases, blindly following their prices draws you away from the optimal market price (equilibrium price that is based on real supply and demand) and can actually drive your RevPAR down in many cases. This is why, in order to make optimal pricing decisions, you need to have access to on-demand **internal hotel data**, such as: the number of vacant rooms by room type, how many groups you have on the books, Out of Order (OOO) rooms, your overselling capacity, the booking pace, etc. Having this will help you consider your property's specifics and adjust your strategy accordingly, as well as recognize the real demand flow that is affecting your particular hotel.

So, how exactly do you use your internal data to assess demand? Many independent and brand hotels still view occupancy as an indicator for increasing or decreasing room rates. A Property Management Systems (PMS) alert may look like this:

"On July 4, 2018 your occupancy reached 70%, you need to increase your rates by $10".

And when you see this, the temptation to follow along can be overwhelming. But you need to stop yourself at this point, because making pricing decisions based on occupancy alone is absolutely incorrect and can lead to great revenue losses.

Instead, when you're looking at your internal data, demand fluctuations should be measured through your property's booking pace *(pickup dynamics)*, which I'll give you more detail on in just a few pages.

Now that we have described your various data sources, let's discuss which one should prevail. The answer is: **internal property data (when available) has priority over macro-level data.** Here's why:

1. Internal data helps understand true demand fluctuations that are specific to this particular property and reflects its unique characteristics (i.e., location, value, physical number of rooms, market mix, FIT and group volume, etc.).

2. Internal hotel data can be used alone and still help hoteliers achieve great results in terms of YOY RevPAR growth. This can't be said about external market data.

Everything stated above does not eliminate the need to be aware of the external market information in order to have a clear understanding of what is happening in the area/region, and how your property is positioned in it.

This macro level data can be used to provide additional details to help you adjust/correct your pricing decisions when need be. This data is also critical when internal data is not available or not significant enough to be successfully analyzed. This happens quite often at smaller properties.

To conclude: while internal data has a higher priority, both categories are important, and both need to be in the equation when calculating optimal prices that lead to profit maximization for your property.

So, based on this discussion, we can see two major mistakes many hotel managers make when pricing their rooms:

- pricing based on occupancy
- blindly following their competitors

The following chapter discusses these mistakes in more detail.

MISTAKE 1: PRICING BASED ON OCCUPANCY

AS DEFINED EARLIER, occupancy is one of the main indexes used in the science of Revenue Management (along with ADR and RevPAR).

The three main misconceptions about occupancy that are still prevalent in the hotel industry are:

- Occupancy should be the target for maximization
- Occupancy should be forecasted
- Occupancy should be the indicator and trigger for price adjustments

Let's review these misconceptions.

Myth 1: Occupancy as the target for maximization

Many hoteliers still view increasing occupancy as the operational target, disregarding all other aspects of Revenue Management in the process. Unfortunately, higher occupancy may actually lead to lower profits when the increased number of rental units doesn't offset the loss in ADR.

Here is a simple example of that:

> ### Scenario 1:
> A 100 room hotel sells 90 units at a $100 rate, obtaining $9000 in Revenue.

> ### Scenario 2:
> The manager sets a goal to achieve 100% occupancy and drops the rate. The hotel sells 100 units at an $85 rate, making only $8500.

From this simple example, it's clear that occupancy itself should not be the goal, as it always has to be looked at together with ADR.

So here's how you make sure that increased occupancy doesn't push you past a 'tipping point' where you start cutting into your bottom line.

In an elastic market (such as hospitality) increase in one parameter (number of rented units, occupancy) always leads to decrease in the other (ADR), and vice versa. So your first goal in understanding demand is to find the right balance between these 2 indexes, in order to achieve your highest potential profits.

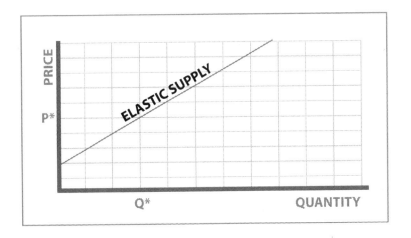

A quick review of your hotel's STR report will help you understand whether your ADR and occupancy are balanced. Ideally, your MPI (occupancy compset index) and ARI (ADR compset index) should be close to each other, at 100% or above.

You don't want to see this:

	Occypancy (%)			ADR			RevPAR		
	My Prop	Comp Set	Index (MPI)	My Prop	Comp Set	Index (ARI)	My Prop	Comp Set	Index (RGI)
Current Month	95.6	87.3	109.6	117.76	136.66	86.2	112.62	119.29	94.4
Year To date	84.7	82.6	102.6	111.12	128.34	86.6	94.12	105.97	88.8
Running 3 Month	84.7	82.6	102.6	111.12	128.34	85.5	94.12	105.97	88.8
Running 12 Month	90.8	78.5	103.0	119.08	127.97	93.1	96.25	100.46	95.8

Or this:

	Occypancy (%)			ADR			RevPAR		
	My Prop	Comp Set	Index (MPI)	My Prop	Comp Set	Index (ARI)	My Prop	Comp Set	Index (RGI)
Current Month	69.4	80.2	86.6	120.91	116.22	104.0	83.95	93.20	90.10
Year To date	70.6	73.6	96.0	112.51	115.85	97.1	79.43	85.24	93.20
Running 3 Month	70.6	73.6	96.0	112.51	115.85	97.1	79.43	85.24	93.20
Running 12 Month	71.8	76.0	94.5	116.84	118.20	98.8	83.89	89.80	93.40

You want to see something like this:

	Occypancy (%)			ADR			RevPAR		
	My Prop	Comp Set	Index (MPI)	My Prop	Comp Set	Index (ARI)	My Prop	Comp Set	Index (RGI)
Current Month	83.9	84.5	99.2	135.42	136.53	99.2	113.63	115.43	98.4
Year To date	74.9	77.7	96.5	120.93	125.19	96.6	90.63	97.25	93.2
Running 3 Month	75.5	77.3	97.7	128.45	129.02	99.6	97.01	99.70	97.3
Running 12 Month	75.2	76.8	97.9	120.67	123.99	97.3	90.70	95.24	95.2

(Note: it's OK if your ADR index is higher than your occupancy index, as long as you're getting your fair share of bookings and your MPI is around the 100 mark).

Now that we've looked at top-line revenues, let's look at a similar situation and pay attention to how your variable costs affect your bottom line (similar to what we discussed earlier in the 'Adjusted RevPAR' chapter).

> ### _Scenario 1:_
> A 100 room hotel sells 90 units at a $100 rate, obtaining $9000 in Revenue.

> ### _Scenario 2:_
> The same hotel sells 100 units at a $90 rate, making the same amount of money ($9000).

In the second case, the manager set a goal to reach 100% occupancy. While the drop in the ADR was indeed offset by the increased number of rented rooms - the overall hotel profitability was lower due to the increased operational expenses associated with renting more rooms.

Let's show that by assuming that variable expenses, or CPOR (cost per occupied room), are $10. Then:

In Scenario 1: overall profit is $9000 - $900 = $8100
In Scenario 2: overall profit is $9000 - $1000 = $8000

More is contributed to the bottom line when we concentrate on increasing ADR rather than occupancy, again, assuming the loss in occupancy is offset by the gain in ADR (as in our second example). So when you're confronted with a thin choice between higher occupancy or higher ADR, go through this exercise to see which one is best for your bottom line. In many cases, it's better to chase ADR in properties with no additional revenue-generating departments (which most limited-service and middle-tier hotels are). For hotels with significant banquet space, restaurants, spas, etc., additional revenue per room also needs to be taken into account in the calculations, because that variable will offset your CPOR (Cost Per Occupied Room).

In conclusion, **occupancy, itself, is not an indicator of how profitable the hotel is and should not be viewed as a goal for maximization.** Instead, **Revenue Managers should concentrate on increasing revenue, actual profits.** Just by making this simple shift in thinking, you'll be much more in line with where the hospitality industry is going these days, and that will help your property, and your career, be much more successful.

Myth 2: Occupancy should be forecasted

Occupancy forecasts were widely spread (and were effective) years ago when hoteliers set the same price for the whole season (or even the whole year) without fluctuating it. Forecasting occupancy, setting an occupancy target, and measuring a hotel's performance based on achieving this target, was a reasonable technique at that time since occupancy was the only variable that was affected by demand and that directly influenced the amount of the final revenue generated.

However, **forecasting occupancy is useless in the current dynamic market conditions.** The resulting occupancy level is dependent on the Revenue Manager's strategy (to be exact: on the price fluctuations, stay restrictions and channel management decisions).

In addition, a particular occupancy target (forecast) does not indicate the profitability of a hotel as there's at least one more variable involved, which is ADR. As explained in the examples above, reaching 100% occupancy does not necessarily mean being more profitable if this leads to a greater decline in ADR. There's also the reverse correlation: due to market elasticity, setting prices higher will lead to lower occupancy, and vice versa.

Thus, forecasting occupancy is no longer effective in the current dynamic pricing situation. Instead, **hoteliers need to concentrate on revenue potential based on forecasted level of demand and select the most optimal strategy to maximize the bottom line.**

Myth 3: Occupancy as the indicator and trigger for price adjustments

Many independent and brand hotels still view occupancy as an indicator for increasing or decreasing room rates.

So to reiterate, making pricing decisions based on occupancy alone is absolutely incorrect and can lead to great revenue (and profit) losses. Let me explain why in greater detail.

1. First of all, **your occupancy % needs to be viewed along with the number of remaining days before arrival.** 70% occupancy tomorrow is very different from 70% occupancy 90 days from now, and thus should be treated differently, and trigger different Revenue Management decisions. In the first case you would most likely lower your price to put more heads in your

remaining beds. The second case obviously indicates high pick up outside of the standard booking window, which should logically lead to increasing the room rate in order to capitalize on the high demand.

Thus, 'occupancy alerts' (still widely used, for some reason, in Property Management and even some Revenue Management systems) are meaningless if the number of days out from a particular stay-date are not taken into account.

2. Second, **along with the number of remaining days, a manager should pay attention to the pickup (booking pace)**, which provides better insight into the real demand conditions.

Let's look at another example to make this point clear.

A manager is reviewing the upcoming weekend in order to make a pricing decision, and at that time she sees that occupancy is at 70%.

> *Scenario 1:*
> during the last 7 days occupancy for that weekend has been picking up at a steady pace, about 5% a day, with a jump of 10% since yesterday.

> *Scenario 2:*
> no reservations have been booked for the weekend during the last 7 days, and the hotel received 3 cancellations yesterday, thus the occupancy dropped from 73% to 70%.

In the 2 cases above, since the booking pace is so different, even though occupancy and the number of remaining days are equal, a smart Revenue Manager will reach an opposite conclusion in each.

Scenario 1 describes high demand with strong pick up, which allows for a price increase since the pickup indicates early sell out at the current price. Scenario 2 describes a situation when either the demand is very weak, or the hotel's room rates are too high. Thus, the most logical decision, in this case, would be to lower the rates to stay competitive.

Again, this confirms that **occupancy alone cannot provide enough information for effective Revenue Management decisions.** Price adjustments that are based only on occupancy while ignoring other parameters are in many cases incorrect and can lead to significant losses.

Instead, concentrate on your booking pace, which is an indicator of the demand strength. If you anticipate early sell out (demand exceeds supply) – increase the price. If the pace is too slow – lower the rate slightly and see how it affects your production. Constantly review and constantly re-adjust. I know this sounds like a daunting task but in reality, **all you need is half an hour a day to grow your Revenue by 10-20% or even 30%. And when you do that, you're well on your way to becoming the most important person at your hotel.**

MISTAKE 2: PRICING BASED ON COMPETITION

ANOTHER MISCONCEPTION that is still prevalent among many hotels of all sizes and star ratings is that in order to be priced accurately, one needs to follow their competitors' rates. Unfortunately, large hotel management companies, hotel chains and even some Revenue Management companies can also be included in this list. This is a habit that has been very heavily ingrained in the Hospitality Industry, and breaking this norm is going to take a lot of training and reinforcement.

The general logic behind this thinking is usually as follows: the prices your neighbors are charging for their hotel rooms make up the total supply in your area, thus affecting market conditions.

Overall, there's nothing wrong with this statement. To correctly understand your hotel's position in the market, it's always important to be aware of the rates your competitors are charging for any given day in the future. However, in many cases, **following their prices blindly draws you away from your optimal market price** (based on real supply and demand), and in many cases makes your hotel lose money. When that happens, you might have to sit through a few uncomfortable meetings.

To avoid this, let's first look at how some hotels get hoodwinked into following others, so you can resist going down a similar path:

- Some hotels pick one competitor they consider 'the closest' and come up with a 'magic differential' ("I need to be $20 below the Best Western next door").
- Others, more advanced, calculate an average/median of all the compset prices and follow that value. This method is widely used in Revenue Management modules built into some Property Management Systems.
- Another method is using compset prices to set parameters (the floor and the ceiling) for your hotel's daily rates, which are calculated some other way.

None of these methods will help you optimize your revenues. Or rather, they may seem to work, but in many cases, they will also lead to profit losses.

Let's examine why.

If we want to take the competitors' rates into account directly and base our pricing recommendations on this information, then:

1. *We have to assume that we have selected a proper compset.*

How often does this happen? How would you evaluate whether this particular competitor is indeed in your direct market? Do you just look at the list in your STAR report?

2. *Even if it were possible to pick 'the right compset', we would then have to accept another assumption: the competitors actually know what they're doing (i.e., they're properly following demand fluctuations and are instantly reacting to these fluctuations with accurate and optimal pricing).*

Can you say that about each hotel in your compset? Your competitors are not always skilled in current Revenue Management strategies, and don't always adequately react to changes in demand, especially if they're not using an automated Revenue Management solution. Since that's the case, why should we be following them at all? Why not be smarter? I.e., If our demand is strong and it dictates to raise our prices up to $200, even while everybody else is charging $180, why wouldn't we go ahead and do that? Why would we want to limit ourselves by the decisions of others, who might not be aware of the true demand

in your area, let alone for your hotel, in particular? We don't want to end up in a situation where 'the blind are leading the blind', now do we? That might make you sell out way too early or force you to go down with too many unsold rooms.

3. *Your competitor may have just booked a large group reservation that leads to an increase in price for transient business.*

Obviously, group business can't be considered as part of transient demand since its demand patterns are very different. If your local competitor just booked a large group, for example, their hotel is now, suddenly, twice as small. And with less rooms to fill, they can afford to increase their prices for the remaining inventory. That's good for them. But why would you increase yours if the true transient demand hasn't really changed, and you don't have the same group on the books? This decision might leave your hotel with drastically diminished occupancy rates, right?

4. *Did you know that your true compset constantly changes? It's not the same every day. And this may depend on the day of the week or a particular event.*

With so many OTA websites in the world these days, the travel market has become transparent. Now customers are equipped with a wide range of tools that help them navigate the market of hotel rooms, knowing much more about hotel rates and availability than ever before. And this information significantly alters their view on what properties to consider during their search.

As a result, customers booking on a week day may be selecting among one set of hotels in an area which is closer to the Convention Center, for example, while weekend travelers are looking at properties closer to the beach. If you're on the edge of both markets – and your hotel is considered in both cases – that means your compset is also constantly shifting. Since this is the case, following the wrong competitor at the wrong time, without considering other factors and your internal property dynamics, could be disastrous for your revenues.

5. *Even for the very same arrival day, different market segments are considering different sets of hotels.*

Let's imagine that next Thursday there's a group who's looking to book rooms for a corporate event (i.e., they are looking at hotels with meeting space), and some want to start their weekend early and look at properties near the entertainment district. Since your hotel is in the middle of it all and has a 1000 sq. ft. meeting room, who would you consider your compset for that Thursday?

Just like different days of the week, different types of travelers are looking for different kinds of accommodations at different times. And while it might seem impossible to understand all this at a moment's notice, the conclusion is simple: **we need to think for ourselves, rather than blindly following others.**

All the points above explain why you may have experienced situations when your demand hasn't changed even though the Best Western next door changed their price by $20.

This may have happened for any of the following reasons:

- This is not really your true competitor (at least not on that day)
- Their pricing decision was not based on real demand conditions
- They may have just booked (or cancelled) a large group
- Your hotel is in a more (or less) advantageous position on this particular day
- Your hotel is in a more (or less) advantageous position for a particular market segment that is booking your hotel at the moment

And when any of these things happen, if demand (your demand) hasn't gone down, but you lower your price out of habit, you'll be losing money at the end of the day. Or, vice versa, if you increase your price following a competitor, kicking yourself out of the market, you lose customers. Clearly, neither of these outcomes will help you get what you want in regards to your property and your career.

So, what *do* you do? The answer is simple: **focus on the real demand flow that's coming into your particular hotel and efficiently react to those changes in demand by adjusting your prices accordingly.**

You can do this by putting together a simple spreadsheet that follows your **booking pace (pick-up dynamics)**, like the one below. It reflects speed of sales and gives you a good view of the real state of your hotel's demand fluctuations, over time.

Date	2017 06/11 Wed	2017 06/12 Thu	2017 06/13 Fri	2017 06/14 Sat	2017 06/15 Sun	2017 06/16 Mon	2017 06/17 Tue	2017 06/18 Wed	2017 06/19 Thu	2017 06/20 Fri	2017 06/21 Sat
Pickup dynamics											
1 days	6	11	11	10	6	6	5	7	9	4	4
7 days	36	26	19	25	22	15	14	14	15	12	17
14 days	51	38	26	32	26	23	23	25	25	16	22
30 days	65	46	31	37	32	31	31	31	29	22	24

Or, if you don't have time to do this, consider using an automated Revenue Management solution that does a good job of tracking this data.

Now, everything stated above does not eliminate the need to be aware of the competitors' prices in order to have a clear understanding of what's happening in the market, and how your property is positioned in it.

But just make sure you're not blindly following your competitors' rates. Again, being an effective Revenue Manager, means you should be closely following the true demand for your hotel and efficiently reacting to the changes in this demand. Whatever the factors affecting demand are (compset rates, weather, gas prices, etc.), they will all be reflected in those demand fluctuations.

STEP 2:
SETTING STAY RESTRICTIONS

IN ADDITION TO DYNAMIC PRICING FLUCTUATIONS, there are a few other non-pricing methods you can use to increase revenue and profits. One method is setting stay restrictions and controls, which help you maximize revenue potential through managing peak and shoulder days. The 2 main restrictions used in the hotel industry are:

Minimum length of stay (MLOS)

This is a restrictor that requires that a reservation is made for at least a specified number of consecutive nights. It allows you to develop a relatively even occupancy pattern during high demand periods or special events. Specifically, this helps keep an occupancy peak on one day from reducing occupancy on shoulder dates.

MLOS can also be applied with discount rates. For example, guests may have to pay Rack rates for shorter stays but they can enjoy a discount for longer stays.

Closed to arrival (CTA)

This keeps guests from arriving on a specified date. You would use this in 2 cases:

1. To limit the number of arrivals on a given day (to reduce the burden on your front desk, for example, in preparation for a large group arrival), and
2. In conjunction with MLOS restrictions to achieve even occupancy during peak demand dates which are longer than 1 night. See an example of this below.

In general, stay restrictions allow hotels to filter less profitable clients during peak demand seasons, thus increasing the resulting room revenue. **It is important to note that they should only be used when estimated sales flow is sufficient enough to reach high occupancy without the loss of revenue.** And it's a good idea to conduct daily audits to make sure you have properly removed those restrictions when that's no longer true.

Let me give you an example of these controls in action.

> ***Example:***
> *There is a 4-day conference that fills all hotel rooms in the city and nearby areas. Since you know for sure your hotel will sell out, as demand significantly exceeds supply - if you don't set any stay restrictions, then 1 or 2 of these 4 days may fill up sooner than the others, thus leaving your shoulder dates unsold. And these shoulder dates will be harder to sell, as they now become a product for a different target audience. I.e., these rooms will only be good for guests who are looking to stay for 1 or 2 nights, with lower price expectations, instead of the much more valuable convention attendee who comes to town for a 4-day event and is ready to pay a higher price.*

That's why we need to apply stay restrictions well in advance. If you do this, then all days in the chain will be sold evenly and at the same high price (assuming you're employing the correct pricing policy and accurately managing demand levels and booking pace). This will allow for maximizing your revenue and profit.

In the following example, the CTA is set along with MLOS, as this is a multiple-night event. We do that because setting just a MLOS for all 4 days won't prevent customers from checking in on any one of the 4 days, and thus won't guarantee even occupancy throughout the whole event.

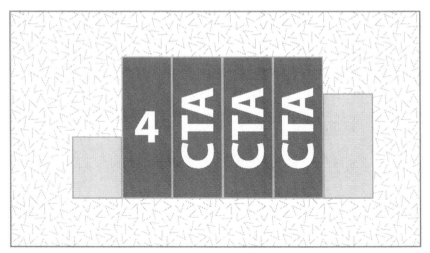

In the second example, when there is only 1 day where booking pace significantly exceeds the shoulder days, a 2-day MLOS restriction is most often used (i.e., on a Saturday night to assist with increasing occupancy for Friday and Sunday).

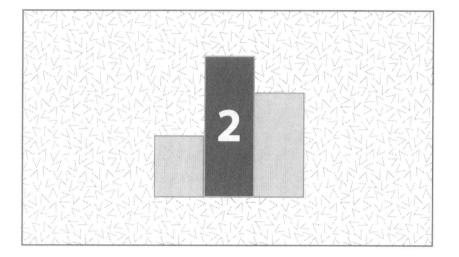

STEP 3:

MANAGING BOOKING CHANNELS

THERE ARE VARIOUS BOOKING CHANNELS

through which a property does its pricing distribution (direct bookings, walk-ins, online travel sites, travel agencies, opaque channels, corporate contracts, etc.). The purpose of booking channel management is to maximize your revenues by restricting some distribution channels with different profitability margins, at different times.

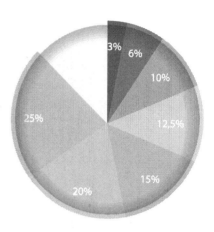

The concept:

Different distribution channels should be configured into a small number of groups, each managed simultaneously. During high demand, it may be beneficial to close less profitable channels in order to maximize the resulting yield. This will slow down the booking pace but will increase the resulting room revenue via the ADR growth.

How it works:

Booking channels are often reflected in a hotel's Property Management System (PMS) through Rate Plans. Many of these rate plans are manageable (i.e., can be closed or open at a specific point in time for a specific date range). For effective Revenue Management, it is important to have a full list of all rate plans with corresponding margins and discounts off your Rack rate (also known as 'the BAR rate'), then group them into 3 or 4 categories based on their profitability level (or, their 'proximity' to Rack rate). After that, manage these **by closing the more expensive (and least profitable) channels when demand and booking pace is high. Then sit back and watch your ADR go up during the high demand periods, which leads to a proportional increase in your profits.**

Let me give you an example of effective Channel Management (CM):

> **_Example:_**
> Let's imagine that a hotel has 6 different rate plans (this is obviously simplified for the sake of the example, as we know in real life this number can go up to 20-30 or even 50 in many cases).
> The rate plans are: RACK, AAA (5% off Rack), AP (15% off Rack promo), OTA (20% off Rack), OPAQUE (30% off Rack), LASTMIN (35% off Rack).
>
> Looking at these rate codes, one can see they're not equal in the size of contribution to the bottom line profits. With that in mind, let's group these plans into 3 different categories, based on their profitability level (from the least expensive and most profitable channels to the most expensive and least profitable):
>
> RACK, AAA – group #1
> AP, OTA – group #2
> OPAQUE, LASTMIN – group #3

When this exercise is done, simply start managing your channels by closing groups #3 and #2 for those dates where you can sell your rooms via group #1 alone, without having to offer deeper discounts. I.e., if your weekends always sell out, you may try to restrict group #3 from booking those dates and see how this affects your occupancy and resulting ADR. For higher demand dates (special events) you can close groups #3 and #2 altogether. Group #1 will always remain open.

Make sure to check back periodically for cases when the channels need to be re-open, if real demand turns out to be slower than anticipated.

There's one more thing to keep in mind as you open and close these various booking channels. In some cases, you may be unwilling to close a particular rate code, due to contracts with different companies that require Last Room Availability, or brand policies, etc. Place those in category #1, which is not closeable. Everything else should be split among your other categories, according to profit margins, and managed as described above.

YOUR FIRST 3 STEPS FOR OPTIMIZING REVENUES, VISUALIZED

We just discussed how to set up your

- Dynamic Pricing strategy
- stay restrictions
- and the proper way to manage your distribution channels

These are the most important items in this book, because they have the highest effect on RevPAR.

Below, I've put together a visual, which will help you see how these 3 'levers' work together, so you can make sure you're using them in a coordinated way to grow your revenues.

This example pertains to a high season event when demand exceeds supply.

Picture a funnel. At the top is everyone who wants to stay at your hotel property, which totals 1,000 potential guests. But you only have 100 rooms to fill, so you can afford to pick and choose between who you are willing to accommodate and who you'll turn away.

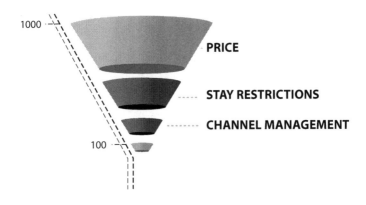

Here's how you make this decision.

Of those 1,000 customers, naturally, they all have different needs and wants, and different price expectations. To begin optimizing your revenues, you first need to **raise your rates** and turn away those who can't meet your price requirements at the top of your funnel.

Second, set **stay restrictions** and only accept those guests who, for example, are willing to stay 2 or more nights, thus narrowing down the field even further.

Last, implement **Channel Management** to make sure no one books through opaque sites or other channels that carry high discounts and hefty commissions.

And there you go! You have just successfully implemented the first 3 steps of optimizing your revenues. You're now left with the 100 most profitable customers of all those who were knocking on your door, which results in your highest potential profit.

This exercise should be completed for every single high-demand date on your calendar. For low-demand dates, you do just the opposite: open all channels, remove stay restrictions, and drop your rates to be more competitive.

STEP 4:
OVERSELLING

OVERSELLING (OR OVERBOOKING) IS A TECHNIQUE used in Revenue Management to offset anticipated cancellations and no-shows. In other words, if you expect 2 cancellations and 1 no-show - you oversell by 3. That's the optimal strategy for maximizing your revenue.

Still, even as simple as this idea is, not very many hoteliers wholeheartedly embrace this practice. In fact, it's very common for most managers (especially in the middle-tier segment) to close out availability on all channels even before they reach the 100% occupancy mark for a certain day. In most cases, this decision is dictated by the fear of dealing with this:

That's a pity, because correctly implemented overbooking practices minimize the chance of 'a walk' while leading to a noticeable increase in revenues (as well as profits). And one doesn't need to have a lot of Revenue Management experience or knowledge to be able to achieve this goal.

In this chapter, I will describe some of the overbooking techniques and best practices that can be used to drive revenues during periods of high demand. My goal here is to show that overbooking is definitely an underestimated strategy. It's also not as scary as it may seem.

Two types of overbooking techniques

The frightening image of a walked guest generally occupies the minds of those who strongly disagree with overbooking as a strategy. But that fear usually comes from a bad past experience when they probably **picked the wrong time to overbook**. Let's look at why this might have happened.

As mentioned above, overbooking is designed to offset cancellations and no-shows. Let's ask ourselves: what is the main difference between those two occurrences? Timing, right?

- *Cancellations* can happen at any point in time, starting from 56 weeks before arrival (the standard allowed lead time for transient bookings) until the end of the cancelation deadline
- *No-shows*, however, always happen on the last day

Thus, we need 2 separate overbooking techniques: one to address cancelations and one to address no-shows.

The latter is easy: calculate the anticipated number of no-shows (using historical data) and overbook on the last day by that many rooms. There are a number of good articles written on this subject (for example, I would recommend you read *"Overbooking Ratio Step-by-Step"* by eCornell).

But! What do we do with cancellations? There are articles explaining how to calculate the average anticipated number of cancelations, but no one tells you WHEN to do this; at what point in time. This is a small, but very important detail!

Timing is the key

> ### *Example #1: bad timing*
> Let's say you're planning your overbooking strategy for the 4th of July this year. You look at your last year's performance report for the same day and discover you had a total of 15 cancelations. Now, that's the final number but it doesn't describe at what point in time those cancellations happened. So, if you're doing this exercise 3 days before arrival and you've just allowed the hotel to oversell by 15 rooms, chances are, you're going to be in this unenviable situation:
>
>
>
> ...simply because you didn't take timing into account.

So here's the key:

It is not enough to just calculate the total number of rooms to oversell. You need to build a curve describing the forecasted number of potential cancellations at any point in time, leading up to the day of arrival. This is very easy to do (see the example below for explanations).

Example #2: Informed timing

This is an example of how you can build a curve of forecasted number of cancellations related to the number of days before arrival. Start with a simple Excel spreadsheet. The forecasted number of potential cancellations can be calculated as the average of actual cancellations from similar days in the past. So your table might look like this:

Days before arrival	1	2	3	4	5	6	7	8	9	10...
The accumulated # of forecasted cancellations	0	1	1	2	2	3	4	4	4	5...

The example above shows 1 to 10 days before arrival, but you should extend yours to at least the number of days that is equal to your average booking window.

As you can see in this example, you shouldn't worry if you find yourself overbooked by 5 rooms 10 days out. However, if you're looking at tomorrow's occupancy (1 day out), you should allow no more than 1 overbooking (unless you also anticipate no-shows).

And another trick:

Overselling needs to happen at the peak of demand, in order to maximize your revenue to its highest potential.

This will ensure that:

a. you sell those rooms at the highest possible price
b. and (in many cases) you still have plenty of time to wait for those precious cancellations (assuming the peak of demand for that day doesn't fall on the last day before arrival, which in most cases it does not)

Proper overselling at the peak of demand helps hoteliers sell their rooms at the premium rate and not leave money on the table from empty rooms due to anticipated cancellations and no-shows.

Now, what exactly do I mean by 'peak of demand'?

Demand is a curved line, it is not even for any day you're selling in the future. Here's a good exercise: pick one day from last year (4th of July, for example) and track the number of reservations booked per day, starting from 365 days before arrival. You may get something like this:

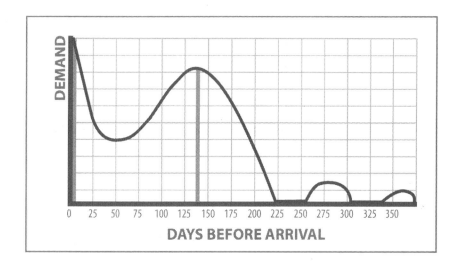

Obviously, we're talking about high demand days only (when you expect to sell out), so there's only that many days that you would need to review for your property. You can use an excel spreadsheet to build this graph if you don't have any automated Revenue Management tool to help you do this.

The graph above describes the actual demand flow for the busiest convention in San Diego – Comic Con that brings about 140,000 visitors every year. The curve is similar for the majority of the city-wide conventions in San Diego.

You would notice 2 peaks: one about 140 days out, and the other one a few days before arrival.

It is also important to understand that price elasticity (and thus, price expectation) is not constant, either; it's also curved. For this event, note how the highest price expectations happen right around the same time as the first peak in demand, and then it goes down.

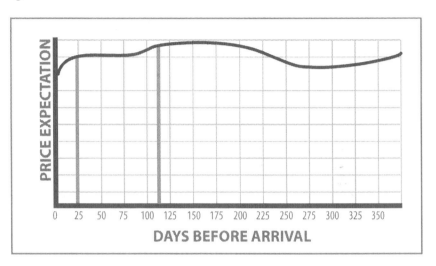

With this correlation, we see that, regardless of the fact that the second peak of demand is higher – the most profitable bookings for this event can be captured 3-4 months out. This is when the majority of the reservations (including oversells) need to happen in order to maximize profits.

> ### *Example #3*
> Here is another example, for better understanding.
> In this example, I want you to imagine there is a hotel with 2 Revenue Managers and they're doing a test to figure out, which booking strategy is best at maximizing their revenues for an upcoming event. For the sake of simplicity, let's assume that demand is similar in both cases.

Here are their results:

	Scenario 1		CxI/NS	Denials	Scenario 2	
Days out	Rate	Availability			Rate	Availability
Final (after day closed)	159	3	3NS		259	0
Same day	159	4			259	-3
1 day out	159	5	1		259	-2
2	159	6			259	-3
3	179	7			259	-3
4	179	7	1		259	-3
5	199	6	2		259	-4
6	199	4	1		259	-6
7	209	3	2		259	-7
8	209	1	1		259	-9
9	239	0		2	259	-10
10	239	0		4	259	-8
11	239	0		4	239	-4
12	239	1			239	1
13	239	5			239	5
14	229	11			229	11
15	229	15			229	15
16	229	17			229	17
17	219	21			219	21
18	219	25			219	25
19	209	29			209	29
20	199	35			199	35

As you can see, manager 1 doesn't like to oversell and declines reservations on days 9, 10 and 11, while manager 2 understands overselling and uses this technique to his advantage, resulting in drastically improved revenues.
Let's take a closer look at the numbers to see why that is.

With this event, the peak of demand and price expectation fell on the 9th, 10th and 11th day before arrival.

Under Scenario 1, the manager closes availability on all channels during those 3 days, unwilling to oversell. This leads to a total of 10 denials that could have been booked at a premium rate. After that, when demand decreases (this may happen for various reasons, i.e., convention hotels releasing their group blocks thus increasing the supply in the market, or competitive hotels lowering their rates pursuing 100% occupancy), booking pace slows down and cancelations start coming in (which is inevitable). Thus, the first manager is forced to respond to the slowing demand conditions with the lower rate in order to avoid going down with too many empty rooms. This manager then aims towards full occupancy and would have been able to achieve it at the end, if not for the 3 no-shows. As a result, 3 rooms remain unoccupied.

One doesn't need to have a CRME certificate to understand that this strategy is far from optimal and leads to significant revenue losses.

In Scenario 2, the hotel is not closed out at the peak of demand and a total of 10 rooms are booked over capacity at the premium $239-$259 rate (i.e., denials turn into actual reservations), anticipating future cancelations and no-shows. This strategy allows the second manager to achieve 100% occupancy as a result. What we also see is that under scenario 2, the manager is not forced to lower the rate to reach full sell out. Moreover, he even increases it further as the demand stays strong and accepts the guests who were turned away in the first strategy. And the rate remains at $259 until the day is closed.

The estimated amount of lost revenue under Scenario 1 is about **$1,750** (considering 3 empty rooms and a lower ADR for the final reservations), compared to scenario 2. And this is just for 1 day. For a 4-day event, multiply this number by 4 – and you see that the first hotel would suffer **$7,000 in pure revenue loss because they refused to use an overbooking strategy! Multiply this by the number of events in the year and this could add up to a 6-figure number**. And this is just for a 100-room, middle-tier property, which this example is taken from. In a larger hotel, the gains/losses would be proportionally greater.

Now, you should note that if you've planned your pricing strategy correctly, you won't often find yourself in a situation when you're close to 100% occupancy that many days out. But, if you are filling up fast, just like in the example above, overbooking is how you capitalize on high demand instead of dropping rates at the end and undermining your own pricing strategy. After all, I've seen cases on high demand dates where cancellations reached 40-50%. Imagine what would have happened to the bottom line if we hadn't had a pro-active overbooking strategy in place then!

So not only can overbooking help you improve your revenues by maintaining a higher ADR, it also shows guests that you don't drop your rates at the last minute, which encourages them to book earlier. AND, it helps you replace earlier OTA reservations with much more profitable bookings as the arrival date draws near (since you will be using your direct channels to overbook).

All this goes to show that having the wrong overbooking policies (or no overbooking policy at all) is detrimental to your revenues. And it's probably only because of fear, that the industry is so resistant to using this strategy, especially in the limited-service/middle-tier segment. But now that you know how to time your overbookings for periods of high demand, you can be sure you're selling your rooms at premium rates and avoiding revenue loss from empty rooms due to cancelations and no-shows. This is an optimal strategy, which leads to revenue (and profit) maximization. **The additional revenues gained from overselling go straight to your bottom line.**

Now that we've optimized our rates and availability, it's time to make sure we're also making the right choices when it comes to managing group and corporate business.

STEP 5:
MANAGING GROUP AND CORPORATE BUSINESS

BY 'MANAGING GROUP AND CORPORATE BUSINESS' I don't mean the actual sales activities to draw demand through these booking channels (that is the responsibility of your sales department). What I mean is assessing the profitability of these booking channels and managing them to maximize revenue and bottom line profit for your hotel.

To make the right choices, when deciding to accept or reject a piece of group business, we need to run through an exercise called **'displacement analysis'**. We do this by comparing the potential consequences of two alternatives:

1. With the first alternative, we calculate the revenue generation from a group request or a corporate contract (which immediately benefits us by adding revenues through rooms sold at a specific negotiated price, plus expected additional revenues generated from other departments).
2. In the second alternative, we make a prediction of the expected sales of the same amount of rooms to transient business (potentially, at a higher price).

Then we compare these two alternatives and find the breakeven price, at the point where the potential revenues from these 2 alternatives are equal. This is the price that we quote to the group or corporate contract. Doing this will allow us to always pick the strategy that will yield higher revenues for the hotel.

This means that, in order to improve profitability, sometimes it's necessary to limit (or decline) a piece of group business for one of the following reasons:

1. Your transient booking channels don't assume such deep discounts, which are normally offered to groups (resulting in a higher ADR)
2. You free yourself from the risk of a potential cancellation of a large number of rooms (this risk still exists, even if you set strict group cancellation rules)

For these reasons, every group or corporate request needs to be analyzed in order to assess its revenue potential against the displacement of expected transient business.

Here's how you would go about making this determination.

As always, let's use a simplified example.

> ### *Example*:
> *Imagine a 100-room hotel. There is a group, which is looking to book 30 rooms for 2 nights on the 4th of July weekend, which historically has been a high demand season. The hotel is already 60% occupied and the current Rack rate is $229 a night.*
>
> *Again, if you don't have any automated tools to assist you with the displacement analysis, you need to calculate your breakeven price. Do this by comparing the potential total revenue generated by the group with the revenue potential through the transient channel for the same amount of rooms.*

> *I.e., If you expect to sell all the remaining rooms at $229 Rack (minus commissions and discounts), then your resulting transient ADR may be somewhere around $200.*
>
> *Multiply that by the number of rooms and number of days: [$200 x 30 x 2 = $12,000]. This is what the **total group value** would need to be in order to equally displace the transient business.*
>
> *Then, subtract the expected revenues generated by other departments that will be applicable to this group, like meeting space or Food and Beverages (FAB). In this example, let's use a $1,000 meeting space fee total for 2 days. With that we see the pure room revenue that needs to be achieved: [$12,000 - $1,000 = $11,000].*
>
> *Divide that by the total number of room nights and we come up with the **breakeven price** to quote per room night: [$11,000 / 60 = $183.33]*
>
> *If the group's asking price is much lower than this rate, then most likely you will be losing revenue by accepting this business and turning away your transient customers.*

One more thing to consider in your analysis is the **wash factor**. As we know, in most cases groups only end up picking up a portion of their block, so make sure to have proper cancellation/cutoff policies in place and keep that expectation in mind when calculating displacement.

It's also important to mention that managers need to look at the bigger picture and sometimes **accept** an unprofitable request, in order to maintain a good relationship with a returning client.

The number of days in your calendar year, for which it may be more beneficial to **decline** a group request or set blackouts for a corporate contract depends on the type of a property, its location, mix of business, and overall market dynamics.

STEP 6:
MARKETING

OBVIOUSLY, MARKETING IS A WHOLE SEPARATE DISCIPLINE and larger hotel properties (or hotel management companies) normally have a separate position (or even a whole department) dedicated to marketing strategies. However, I feel obligated to list it here because marketing needs to go hand in hand with Revenue Management, since your demand seasons, rates and availability will, ultimately, determine what campaigns you run and when.

One of the biggest dreams of any hotelier is **to be able to shift business away from the OTAs to the hotel's direct sales channels** (which we know are the least expensive for hotels and thus the most profitable). The truth is, however, it's hard to accomplish just through the use of Revenue Management techniques alone, which is why larger hotel operations will have separate marketing and sales departments to help their Revenue Manager achieve this goal.

Unfortunately, not everyone has these luxuries. And there are many times when I've had to take care of my properties' marketing efforts.

In the following section, I'd like to share a few strategies that will help you navigate your production towards your hotel's direct booking channel and win your fair share of the market.

Pre- and post-stay communication

As an example, this can include automated emails to guests before their arrival (promoting the property's additional services, offering upgrades, etc.) and after their departure (enticing the customers to return to the property in the future in exchange for a discount or a free add-on, for example).

Social Media marketing

Every hotel property needs to represent itself on Facebook, Instagram, Twitter (and the list goes on). These accounts need to be managed to be effective (meaning that content needs to be posted at least once a week, and all guest messages need to be responded to). When managed properly, these platforms can help get your property in front of your target audience to generate demand for need dates and navigate business to your website. Targeted paid campaigns on these platforms can also be very effective.

Email marketing

This is one of the most effective and least expensive hotel marketing strategies there is. You can export your guest database from your Property Management System (you own the data, after all!) and use it to send out periodic e-blasts with attractive offers. Don't overdo it though, as people will be quickly unsubscribing if you start bombarding them with spam on a weekly basis. A rule of thumb is one email per month (or less often), which ideally should correspond with special events or holidays.

Traditionally, these campaigns have been used to generate demand during slow periods. However, the trick is that these promotions are even more effective during high demand dates.

Consider this: your average OTA commission is probably about 20%, which on a slow date can translate to $10-$20. But on a peak date, you could be giving away nearly $100 with each reservation an OTA books for you. Thus, **the return from those e-marketing campaigns is much higher during high demand dates, because they help you steal your guests back from third parties.** So, even if you have to offer a small discount or a value-add in return – it's still very advantageous to run promotions during these times.

PPC campaigns

This is pretty self-explanatory. If you have a marketing budget – try running paid campaigns on the search engines and track results. There's one exception to this strategy, however. I do not recommend running PPC ads on the OTAs since this contradicts the concept of trying to shift business away from your most expensive channels.

I also would like to emphasize **the importance of properly coding all your campaigns and carefully tracking results,** in order to be able to calculate your ROI from each. And there's no other way to know which tactic turned out to be the most effective and which one(s) you need to drop. For this, you absolutely need **Google Analytics hooked up to your website.** If you're not much of a technical person, just hire an IT guy who will do it in a second. This will also help you understand, which audiences to target in your marketing campaigns, improving your conversions and lowering your costs even more.

OTHER TACTICS FOR INCREASING REVENUE

THERE ARE A FEW OTHER THINGS Revenue Managers can do to increase their hotel's productivity. When you've mastered everything described above, go ahead and add the following items to your daily routine, as well.

Managing online reviews

TripAdvisor is the undisputed leader in the world of online travel reviews. According to TripAdvisor (in 2015):

- 96% of users consider reading reviews important when planning trips and booking hotels.
- 83% of users will 'usually' or 'always' reference reviews before deciding to book a hotel.
- More than half of users will not book a property that doesn't have any reviews.

This is why it's so important to keep an eye out for (and respond to) positive and negative reviews on all your sales and marketing channels, such as: TripAdvisor, your own website (if you have this functionality), all major OTA sites, as well as social media platforms.

Here are some additional reasons you should get involved with reputation management:

1. This will help you improve different areas of operations (through identifying opportunities for improvements).
2. You'll be able to report fake reviews (which are dragging your score, and revenues, down) and have them removed.
3. You'll increase your visibility across social media and booking platforms.
4. By showing you care, you increase customer loyalty.
5. This will draw more traffic to your website.
6. A good reputation helps you maintain your competitive advantage.
7. And all this increases your RevPAR and helps shift business away from the OTAs.

So spend a little time on this each day and reap the rewards for years to come.

Upgrading

Upgrading is also an effective way of increasing revenues. Make an attempt to sell additional services or amenities at the front desk, on your website or via email marketing campaigns. A caller/booker may be unaware of varying rates and amenities, for example, so employees must be trained to listen to guests and make suggestions for an appropriate accommodation or service.

There are also software tools that can help you maximize your revenues through proper upselling. So spend a little time figuring out what's right for you, put a policy in place and then track your results over time to figure out how you can use upgrading as part of your total Revenue Management strategy.

Managing room type differentials

Different room types may have different demand patterns, so it's good to keep an eye on them separately. Do this by watching the booking pace of different room types during different demand seasons and increase (or decrease) the difference between them to maximize revenue results.

For example, during the summer season, your 2-bedroom suites may be more popular if your hotel attracts family business. But then you might find you get more corporate clientele (single-bed users) during the winter.

Here's a simple way to analyze it. You can look for a "Room Type Analysis" report in your Property Management system, though this is not widely available. If your PMS doesn't offer this – you can build a report yourself using the example below. First, calculate the average occupancy per room type over a 12-month period, then do the same exercise by month to see if the results change based on the season.

Let's look at this example from a real 47-room property to see what this might look like and draw conclusions.

Type	Count	Sold	To sell	ADR	RevPAR	Revenue	Occ
BV1K	1	31	31	104	104	3,224.00	100.00%
BV2Q	7	193	217	76.19	67.76	14,704.27	88.94%
OV1K	3	81	93	79.7	69.41	6,455.55	87.10%
OV2Q	5	136	155	87.56	76.83	11,908.35	87.74%
OVSU	4	84	124	94	63.68	7,895.85	67.74%
PS1K	1	31	31	104	104	3,224.00	100.00%
PS2Q	7	177	217	81.34	66.34	14,396.65	81.57%
PV1K	2	55	62	84.47	74.93	4,645.65	88.71%
PV2Q	6	151	186	85.82	69.67	12,958.37	81.18%
PVSU	4	91	124	118.81	87.19	10,811.55	73.39%
ST1K	1	20	20	50	50	1,000.00	100.00%
ST2Q	6	151	186	79.42	64.48	11,992.65	81.18%
		1,201	1,446	85.94	71.38	103,216.89	83.06%

In the table above, we can see there are 3 room types that are always sold out (during the given date range): BV1K, PS1K, ST1K. This means that the prices for those can be increased to capitalize on the ADR.

There are also 2 room types that are running at relatively low occupancy: OVSU and PVSU, which happen to be suites. This most likely means the hotel is overcharging for those, so it would be a good idea to slightly decrease the differential to be able to increase production from those two room types.

Managing ancillary revenues

Many hotels have other revenue-generating departments, in addition to rooms. If those revenues are significant, it is also important to manage them to maximize overall profitability of the hotel. Sometimes, this may mean discounting (or even eliminating) the charge of one department to increase the revenue from another one, thus increasing the overall bottom line. Example: offering free parking or a restaurant discount as an incentive for booking a large group.

REVIEW

BELOW, I'VE LISTED THE DIFFERENT TACTICS you should put in place to maximize your hotel's revenues during periods of high and low demand. Just follow these steps, one-by-one, and you'll be well on your way to becoming the in-demand Revenue Manager that everyone's talking about.

Strong demand tactics (work hard, capitalize on ADR!)

1. Increase your Rack/BAR rate (which will, in turn, increase the rate for all derived rate plans)
2. Apply Closed To Arrival (CTA), Minimum Length of Stay (MLOS) and other restrictions
3. Close or restrict less profitable channels (this can include discounts as well as rate plans with high margins)
4. Oversell by a necessary amount at the peak of demand
5. Reduce group room allocations
6. Reduce or eliminate 6 P.M. holds (if any)
7. Tighten your guarantee and cancellation policies
8. Increase rate difference between room types, apply full price to suites and executive rooms
9. Steal production away from OTAs by running marketing campaigns, thus growing your ADR by increasing your Net rate and avoiding commissions

Weak demand tactics (work even harder, increase occupancy!)

1. Run marketing campaigns to increase demand
2. Remove any stay restrictions
3. Keep all discounted channels open
4. Offer promos and packages
5. Remove any limits from group room allocations and release blackouts from corporate accounts
6. Encourage upgrades (move guests to a better accommodation or class of service to enhance their experience and encourage them to come back again)
7. Involve your staff (create an incentive contest to increase occupancy)
8. Lower your rates

AUTOMATION IN HOSPITALITY REVENUE MANAGEMENT

AS WE HAVE BEEN DISCUSSING throughout this book, Revenue Management decisions (pricing and others) are based on analysis of vast amounts of information on: booking pace, booking history, compset rates, hotels' parameters and specifics, and other variables. Although many individual tasks of Revenue Management can be performed manually, the most efficient way to handle data and generate profits is through Revenue Management Software (RMS). That's why many hoteliers choose to employ specialized computer programs dedicated to Revenue Management automation.

So, just like every store uses a cash register to improve the speed, efficiency and accuracy of their commerce, I strongly recommend you put some kind of Revenue Management Software in place to facilitate your strategic decision making.

Just know that hotel Revenue Management Systems (RMS) vary greatly. On one side, for example, there are strictly informative/analytical systems that will only perform functional data presentations on your computer (or tablet) screen. On the other, there are systems that are able to make final decisions in a completely automated mode, based on sophisticated algorithms of modeling, forecasting and optimization. They may include elements of artificial intelligence and methods of adaptation (customization) to a hotel's specific characteristics. And others are positioned somewhere in between.

It will take a little while for you to get a clear understanding of all these options and decide which is best for your particular property. But I say that's time well spent. Because anything that helps you do your job faster, more efficiently and with greater precision will, ultimately, produce a return on investment in just a few months.

Benefits of an automated Revenue Management System

1. The effectiveness of Revenue Management actions (in setting Dynamic Pricing in particular) is greatly increased with an RMS. Using an automated Revenue Management System can lead to a 10-15% revenue increase in general (or higher in some cases).
2. For hotels that spend too much time on 'manual' management, an RMS system will allow them to lower their payroll expenses.
3. It also allows you to eliminate significant errors in pricing decisions, especially in conditions of economic instability.
4. Such systems also help managers save time on routine analytical tasks so they can concentrate on more important, strategic decisions.

Altogether, an RMS system can make your worklife a lot better, and your hotel – a lot more profitable. And isn't that what being a next-level Revenue Manager is all about?

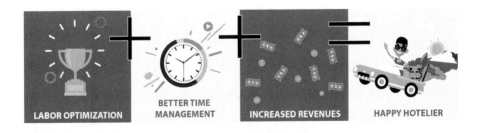

LABOR OPTIMIZATION + BETTER TIME MANAGEMENT + INCREASED REVENUES = HAPPY HOTELIER

SUMMARY

IF YOU WANT TO BECOME the most important person at your hotel, these are the main areas of revenue optimization that you need to master.

1. Dynamic Pricing

Make sure to keep an eye on your booking dynamics and competitive environment so you can always adjust your prices accordingly. Every few hours – check stats for the nearest 1-2 days. Every day – review the number of days in the future that is equal to your average booking window. Review the rest of the year at least once a week. At the end of the month – smile as you watch your RevPAR index grow by 10-20-30%.

2. Setting (and removing) stay restrictions

Review all high demand dates in the future and set MLOS and CTAs and other restrictions that you may want to use when appropriate. Do this for both: dates that are forecasted to be busy (known special events) and dates that are already picking up ahead of pace. Make sure to record all restrictions and review them periodically so you can remove them later if demand slows down.

3. Managing your booking channels

Review all dates in the future. Make sure all channels are open for slow demand seasons (by 'season' I don't mean summer, fall, winter and spring... each day should be treated as a separate season). Close the most expensive (least profitable) channels for high demand dates in order to increase Net rate. Again, make sure to keep a record so you can adjust your decisions later if needed.

4. Using overselling when appropriate

When demand exceeds supply and your booking pace indicates early sell out (hopefully you have also increased your rates and used all other high-demand tactics that we discussed previously, so you don't sell out too early) – allow yourself to oversell by the appropriate number of rooms to take advantage of the peak of demand and price expectation. But make sure to take into consideration the number of days before the event in question. This will help you estimate your number of anticipated cancelations.

5. Properly managing group and corporate business

Have a list of blackout dates handy (high demand event dates that you wouldn't be willing to offer at a discounted rate). Always review your transient rates and booking dynamics before quoting a group rate to make sure you don't displace more profitable transient business during that same time. Also remember to apply proper cancelation and cutoff policies (the larger the group – the longer the cutoff and cancelation window should be). This will help you avoid situations when you end up with 50% of inventory unsold just a few days before arrival – without enough time to resell those rooms through other channels.

6. Implementing basic marketing tactics

Stay in touch with the marketing department and make sure they are aware of the slow and high demand seasons and all future blackout dates. If there is no marketing department, implement a few basic marketing tactics yourself to draw demand during slow seasons and increase Net rate during high seasons. Start with Social Media and email campaigns using inexpensive platforms like Constant Contact or MailChimp.

And then there are a few additional areas of opportunity you should explore after you've mastered the basics.

These include:

Reputation Management

Keep an eye on the online reviews people leave for your hotel on channels, such as: Trip Advisor, the OTAs and various Social Media platforms. Analyze those reviews to pinpoint problems with your customer service or the property's physical condition, and then make improvements, if possible. Respond to reviews and effectively turn complaints into advertising.

Upgrading

Offer upgrades and promote additional services to generate more revenue.

Managing room type differentials

Analyze production by room type and adjust differentials if needed. Fluctuate them according to seasonal changes in demand (increase rates for more expensive room types and suites during busy dates).

Managing ancillary revenues

Analyze all revenue generating channels and manage them the way that would maximize your hotel's overall profitability.

Automating

There have been an increasing number of great tools available in the market that help hoteliers become more efficient, productive and profitable. And every year more and more technology startup companies appear on the hospitality horizon. If you decide to automate any part of your hotel's operations, I would suggest attending a HITEC tradeshow to become more familiar with your options.

TO CONCLUDE, the goal of this book was to **describe the main Revenue Management techniques that are relevant in hospitality today**, in simple language, with clear and easy-to-understand examples. This way, any small- or mid-tier hotel can make Revenue Management a part of their everyday operations, and confidently add an extra 10-20% or even 30% to their revenues every year.

However, if you are new to the discipline, this is probably a lot to digest for now. Don't worry; there is no need to implement every item on this list as soon as you get back to your office tomorrow morning. Just start with the first item and proceed to the next one as you become more comfortable and more confident with your strategy. Naturally, there will probably be some trial and error in the beginning, but it will all become clear very soon. And once you have a routine (I find that half an hour a day is usually enough for an average, midscale hotel) – you'll see it start to get exciting, and that will push you to grow your RevPAR even more!

Good luck with your endeavors and I hope this book has helped you become a more successful hospitality professional!

GLOSSARY

A

Adjusted RevPAR (ARPAR) – a new performance metric that, unlike traditional RevPAR, reflects the bottom line profits and not just the top line revenue. Calculated as follows: ARPAR = (ADR – Var costs per occ room + Add. rev per occ room) x Occupancy

Average Daily Rate (ADR) – average rental income per occupied room in a given time period. Calculated as follows: Room revenue/ Number of rooms sold. Expressed in monetary units.

B

Best Available Rate (BAR) – the lowest non-restricted rate bookable by all guests. This rate can change several times a week and up to several times a day.

Booking Pace – the speed at which bookings materialize over a period of time from the booking date to the arrival date.

Business Mix – the blend of different market segments that occupy a hotel, measured as a value or percent of occupancy.

Business Type – a market segment description of either Group or Transient.

C

Channel Management – provides a way for hotels to control the allocation of hotel inventory and rates across all distribution channels including websites, third parties and the GDS.

Closed to Arrival (CTA) – a stay restriction that does not allow reservations with date of arrival at a specified date.

Competitive Set – comparable hotels in a hotel's vicinity that compete for guests.

Competitor – a hotel's defined competitor for which rates are supplied by an Internet-based rate shopping service and whose rates impact the hotel's pricing strategy.

Constrained Demand – the quantity of rooms that are expected to be sold for a date. Considers limitations such as a hotel's capacity or restrictions on bookings.

Cost of Walk – the cost of turning away a guest when the hotel is unable to provide the promised accommodation, which may include the cost of a hotel room, complimentary gifts, and probable lost future business.

D

Days to Arrival – the number of days prior to an Arrival Date used to measure information such as a booking pace, hotel performance and forecast performance. Demand – strength of business anticipated for future days.

Displacement Analysis – an analysis of business (primarily Group) that is based on the total value of the business versus the value of the transient business that would be displaced if the business were accepted.

F

Fenced – rates a hotel uses to provide a series of options to guests. The rate is determined by which fences a guest accepts, which might include nonrefundable and non-cancelable reservations, advanced purchase reservations, and staying over a weekend.

G

Global Distribution System (GDS) – comprehensive travel shopping and reservation platform that travel agents use to book airline, car, hotel and other travel arrangements for their customers.

Group Blocks – block of rooms intended for bookings at negotiated rates from a limited range of guests.

Group Demand – the group business expected for future days.

Group Wash – the difference between the final occupancy from a group and the maximum value of the block.

I

Inventory – total number of rooms in operation for selected date.

K

KPI – Key Performance Indicators, for example: Average Daily Rate (ADR), Revenue per Available Room (RevPAR), Occupancy.

L

Length of Stay (LOS) – the number of nights a guest stays at a hotel, the difference between the departure date and the arrival date.

M

Market Segment – a portion of the customers who possess a common set of motivations as well as a combination of unique purchasing (e.g., advance purchase vs. walk-in) and usage patterns (e.g., single night vs. weekly).

Maximum Length of Stay – a stay restriction that limits the number of nights a reservation can stay when arriving on a certain date.

Minimum Length of Stay – a stay restriction that allows reservations only for at least a specified number of consecutive nights, if this date is a requested arrival date.

Minimum Stay-Through – a stay restriction that allows reservations only for at least a specified number of consecutive nights.

N

No-Show – the case where some customers with a reservation do not show up to use the room(s) reserved for them, without explicit cancellation.

O

Occupancy – percentage of all rental units in the hotel that are occupied at a given time. Calculated as follows: Number of occupied rooms / Number of total available rooms. Expressed as a percentage.

Occupancy Index – the measure of a property's occupancy percentage compared to the occupancy percentage of the competitive set. Calculated as follows: hotel Occupancy/ competitive set Occupancy * 100.

Online Travel Agency (OTA) – an Internet-based hotel and travel reservations system. Hotels typically provide inventory to OTAs, which sell the rooms in exchange for a commission.

Opaque – a booking channel where the supplier (hotel) remains hidden until after the purchase is complete.

Overbooking – the practice of selling more rooms than are physically present in the hotel to account for cancellations and no-shows. The goal of overbooking is to maximize revenue by achieving as close to 100% occupancy as possible on any given day.

Overbooking Limit – allowed number of accepted bookings above inventory.

P

Pace – also called pickup, pace is the rate at which reservations are made for a particular date.

Price Elasticity – an economic measure that shows the responsiveness or 'elasticity' of the demand for a product based on a change in its price.

ProPAR – Profits per Available Room, a metric that calculates net revenue. This factors in customer acquisition costs and other expenses. Also known as Net RevPAR.

Property Management System (PMS) – a system used by hotels to manage operations and to allow for guest check-in and check-out.

Q

Qualified Rate – a rate that the guest must qualify for: i.e., a corporate rate for the guest's company, a rate available due to an affiliation such as AARP, a promotional package rate with specific booking conditions, etc.

R

Rate Shopping – an Internet-based service that supplies competitor rate data to hotels.

Rate Parity – strategy used to maintain consistency of rates between sales channels, usually enforced through contractual agreements between hotel companies and third-party vendors.

Regret – a notification that the hotel has been shopped on its direct booking engine and a rate was given, but a guest chooses not to accept the reservation.

Reputation Management – influencing and controlling of a hotel's reputation online. Originally a public relations term. The growth of the internet and social media, along with reputation management companies, have made search results a core part of a hotel's reputation.

Revenue Management – the art and science of predicting real-time customer demand and optimizing the price and availability of products to match that demand, with the goal to maximize the bottom line profits.

Revenue Management System – software application hotels use to control the supply and price of their inventory in order to achieve maximum revenue or profit, by managing availability, room types, stay patterns (future and historical), etc.

Revenue per Available Room (RevPAR) – a metric used to measure a hotel's productivity and also to compare different properties within a market. Can be calculated in a few different ways:

[ADR x Occupancy], or
[Total guest room revenue / Number of total available rooms / Number of days in the period]

RevPAR Index (RPI) or Revenue Generating Index (RGI) – a metric used to determine whether a property is achieving its fair share of revenue compared to a specific group of hotels (competitive set). It is calculated by taking the RevPAR of the property and dividing it by the RevPAR of the competitive set (competitive set data collected through a third-party provider, such as STR).

Room Block – a group of rooms that may be created to organize rooms to aid in planning, sales or other management tasks. Examples include associating rooms with a single fixed price, a single guest, a channel, a group or a single team of staff members that manage or maintain the rooms in the block.

Room Nights – rooms blocked or occupied multiplied by the number of nights each room is reserved or occupied.

Room Type – a collection of rooms sharing a common element at the hotel.

S

STR – a company that provides a clearing house where hotels can enter their own operating data (ADR, Occupancy and total rooms) and STR then aggregates this information with data from other hotels in the same market and allows participating hotels to compare their KPIs.

Shoulder Dates – nights that are next to full or very compressed dates.
Special Event – period(s) where the transient business pattern is different than normal.

T

Transient Bookings – bookings at public or negotiated rates from guests not associated with a group.

Transient Demand – the anticipated volume of business from transient market segment

U

Unconstrained Demand – demand that is not constrained by the capacity or restrictions of the hotel and could be sold if the hotel had an unlimited number of rooms available to sell.

Unqualified Rates – rates that are offered by the hotel to guests who do not have an agreed contract rate and that have no restrictions or booking conditions attached to them.

W

Wash – the difference between the group block and what the hotel expects it will actually pick up.

Y

Yield Management – sometimes synonymous with Revenue Management, set of strategies that help realize optimal revenues and profits for capacity-constrained and perishable assets. The core concept of yield management is to provide the right service to the right customer at the right time for the right price – by understanding, anticipating and influencing consumer behavior.

Made in the USA
San Bernardino, CA
16 May 2018